THE DHAMMAPADA

BEING

AN ANCIENT ANTHOLOGY PRESERVED IN THE SHORT COLLECTION OF THE SACRED SCRIPTURES OF THE BUDDHISTS

Translated by ALBERT J. EDMUNDS

D0006538

The Dhammapada
Translated by Albert J. Edmunds

Print ISBN 13: 978-1-4209-5424-1
eBook ISBN 13: 978-1-4209-5425-8

Cover Image: The Buddha, c. 1905 (pastel on paper), by Odilon Redon (1840-1916) / Musee d'Orsay, Paris, France / Bridgeman Images.

Please visit *www.digireads.com*

CONTENTS

DEDICATED TO MY FRIENDS

BUNFORD AND ELLA SAMUEL

OF MOUNT AIRY, PHILADELPHIA

AS WHOSE GUEST I TRANSLATED THE

GREATER PART OF THIS BOOK

Introduction

This ancient anthology of Buddhist devotional poetry was compiled from the utterances of Gotamo and his disciples; from early hymns by monks; and from the popular poetic proverbs of India. Several of the *Dhammapada* verses are found in the Hymns by Monks, a book of the sacred Pâli Canon. Others are found scattered throughout that Canon, in all its main collections of Discourses, and four even in the Books of Discipline; while we encounter yet others in the national Epic of India and in the Law-Book of Manu, which is the Hindû Deuteronomy. These last are written in classical Sanskrit; but as Pâli is a popular idiom thereof, but little change is needed to turn a stanza from one tongue to the other—no more than to Anglicize the *Hallowe'en* of Burns. Not only in the pure Sanskrit of the Brahmin classics do we find stray lines of our Hymns, but in the corrupt Sanskrit of later Buddhist literature, which arose in the valley of the Ganges during the two centuries preceding the Christian era. Moreover, some fragments of Buddhist verse found in Chinese Turkestan, and dating from very early times, contain stanzas known to the *Dhammapada*, but written in a debased Prâkrit or provincial dialect.

In these various forms—Pâli, Sanskrit and Prâkrit,[1]—the sacred books were recited in Buddhist monasteries, from Ceylon to Afghanistan, for four hundred years, until, about 40 B. C.,[2] they began to be written; at first in Ceylon alone, but afterwards wherever the religion went. A Chinese account, however, says that the Book of Discipline was copied in the second century B. C., from an older archetype. In the early Christian centuries the Hymns were taken to China, to Cambodia, and still later to Burmah,[3] Japan, Tibet and Siam. We have at least one version in Chinese which sticks quite close to the

---

[1] The Tibetans relate that the Buddhist Scriptures were handed down in Sanskrit and three dialects.

[2] Kern's corrected date.

[3] There was apparently a mission to Burmah in the third century B. C., but we cannot prove its continuity.

Pâli, though adding new selections. Besides this true translation, the Chinese have produced varied recensions (just as the early Christians with the Clementines) which deal very freely with the matter. At the same time, the Chinese had an historical and critical sense which was lacking in the Hindûs, and they knew the difference between a faithful and a licentious textual form. We have appended to this introduction the Chinese preface translated by Beal, the quaint statements of which will bear out what we are saying, and throw light also upon the religious mind of China, which is not essentially different from our own.

As our collection of Hymns is a series of extracts, it is possible that it was not compiled until after the age of writing. So the Chinese Preface would make it appear; but Hindû literary habits and ours are so different, that we cannot be sure of this. The Chinese in other accounts even give the name of the compiler, Dharmatrâta; and some indications seem to point to the first century before Christ as his date. But this is uncertain. We do know, however, both from the Pâli Monkish Hymn-Book, and from the Tibetan historian, that hymn-writers flourished during the third century that followed the demise of Gotamo, as well as earlier.

The first printed edition of the *Dhammapada* was made in 972, when the Chinese recension of the Buddhist Scriptures and their concomitant literature was first printed. The Pâli original was destined to be printed at last by a Christian scholar at Copenhagen in 1855, when Vincent Fausböll's edition was also the first Pâli text to be printed in Europe.[4] It is from this veteran scholar's second edition (London, 1900) that our present translation has been made. Much help has been derived from the Latin translation of Fausböll which accompanies his text; from the English of Max Müller (*Sacred Books of the East*, Vol. X.: Oxford, 1881; second edition, 1898)[5]; and from the French of Fernand Hû (Paris, 1878.) I have not had the fortune to see the German of Weber or the English of James Gray. The literal Latin of Fausböll is especially valuable. For further information, and for the various meanings of the term *Dhammapada*, we refer the reader to Max Müller's Introduction to his translation. Our own rendering of the word is based upon Stanzas 44 and 102 of the work itself, and upon the understanding thereof among the Hindû monks who took the book to China.[6]

---

[4] Spiegel's *Anecdota Pâlica* (1845) were extracts.

[5] First published in 1870.

[6] In Numerical Collection IV., 29, *Dhammapadâni* (the plural *of Dhammapada*) means the "feet of religion." Its four feet are: not coveting, not hating, right collectedness, and right trance. In *Sutta Nipâto* 87, Dhammapada seems to mean "path of religion"; but Fausböll here spells it with a capital, and it looks as if our *Dhammapada* book were being mentioned. This, however, is unlikely.

If ever an immortal classic was produced upon the continent of Asia, it is this. Its sonorous rolls of rhythm are nothing short of inspired; and, while sticking to an almost literal translation, I have tried to convey some flavor of the original by using an archaic and poetic style. Perhaps it is too ambitious a wish to hope to naturalize in English this Buddhist Holy Writ, as the King James version has naturalized the Christian; but if I fail some one else will succeed. No trite ephemeral songs are here, but red-hot lava from the abysses of the human soul, in one out of the two of its most historic eruptions. These old refrains from a life beyond time and sense, as it was wrought out by generations of earnest thinkers, have been fire to many a muse. They burned in the brains of the Chinese pilgrims, who braved the blasts of the Mongolian desert, climbed the cliffs of the Himâlayas, swung by the rope-bridge across the Indus where it rages through its gloomiest gorge, and faced the bandit and the beast, to peregrinate the Holy Land of their religion, and tread in the footsteps of the Master. Verses were graven on the walls of august temples at the command of Hindû emperors who abolished capital punishment, mitigated slavery, and established hospitals for men and animals, under the sway of this marvelous cult; and by Ceylon monarchs whose ruined reservoirs, as large as lakes, astonish us among the wonders of antiquity. And to-day, after twenty centuries of Roman and Christian culture, they have won the admiration of Europeans and Americans in every seat of learning, from Copenhagen to the Cambridges, and from Chicago to St. Petersburgh.

ALBERT J. EDMUNDS.

Historical Society of Pennsylvania: September, 1901.

FA-KHEU-KING TSU

(CODEX I)

Preface to the Sutra Called Fa-Kheu[7]

(LAW-VERSES: DHAMMAPADA)

The verses called Dhammapada (*Tan-poh*) are selections from all the Sûtras. The expression *Tan* means law, and the word *poh* means verse or sentence. There are various editions (or arrangements) of this Dhammapada Sûtra. There is one with 900 verses, another with 700, and another with 500.[8] Now the word for verse, or Gâthâ, signifies an extract from the Scriptures arranged according to metre. These are the words of Buddha himself, spoken as occasion suggested, not at any one time, but at various times, and the cause and end of their being spoken is also related in the different Sûtras. Now Buddha, the All-wise, moved by compassion for the world, was manifested in the world, to instruct men and lead them in the right way. What he said and taught has been included in twelve[9] sorts of works. There are, however, other collections containing the choice portion of his doctrine, such, for instance, as the four works known as the Âgamas.[10] After Buddha left the world, Ânanda collected a certain number of volumes[11] in each of which the words of Buddha are quoted, whether the Sûtra be large or small, with this introductory phrase: "Thus have I heard." The place where the sermon was preached is also given, and the occasion and circumstances of it. It was from these works that the Shamans, in after years,[12] copied out the various Gâthâs,—some of four lines, some of six

---

[7] Translated from the Chinese by Samuel Beal, and reprinted from his edition of the Parable Recension of the Chinese Dhammapada: London, 1878. [The notes are mine. A. J. E.]

[8] Beal points out that these are round numbers. The last is identical with the Pâli number of verses, 423. For, in Buddhist usage, 500 means the fifth hundred. So, when the Chroniclers tell us that the Vesâli schism took place a hundred years after the Master's death, we know that they mean some time during the first Buddhist century.

[9] The twelve *Angâni* or Subjects of the Buddhist Canon, in the Pâli recension nine. They represent the oldest arrangement of the Scriptures.

[10] The Four Collections of *Sûtras* (Pâli *Suttas*) or Discourses. The different sects agree, in the main, as to the Four, but differ about the contents of the Fifth, which, in the Pâli, contains the *Dhammapada*. Even the sect which has transmitted the Pâli Canon does not treat the Fifth or Short collection consistently; for, while the Majjhima reciters canonize it, the older Dîgha reciters put it in the Abhidhammo, which is, from the catholic standpoint, uncanonical.

[11] The Chinese who had had written books for so many centuries, naturally imagined that the Sûtras were written from the first.

[12] Beal elsewhere translates this: "in after ages."

lines,—and attached to each set a title according to the subject therein explained. But all these verses, without exception, are taken from some one or other of the accepted Scriptures, and therefore they are called Law-verses (or Scripture extracts), because they are found in the Canon.

Now the common edition used by the people generally is the one with 700 Gâthâs. The meaning of these Gâthâs is sometimes very obscure (deep), and men say that there is no meaning at all in them. But let them consider that, as it is difficult to meet with a teacher like Buddha, so the words of Buddha are naturally hard of explanation. Moreover, all the literature of this religion is written in the language of India, which widely differs from that of China,—the language and the books, in fact, are those of the Devas (Heaven). So to translate them faithfully is not an easy task.

The present work, the original of which consisted of 500 verses, was brought from India in the third year of the reign of Hwang-wu (A. D. 223),[13] by Wai-chi-lan, and, with the help of another Indian called Tsiang-im, was first explained, and then translated into Chinese. On some objection being made as to the inelegance of the phrases employed, Wai-chi-lan stated "that the words of Buddha are holy words, not merely elegant or tasteful, and that his law is not designed to attract persons by its pleasing character, but by its deep and spiritual meaning."

Finally, the work of translation was finished, and afterwards thirteen additional sections added, making up the whole to 752 verses, 14,580 words, and headings of chapters thirty-nine.[14]

---

[13] In his *Abstract of Four Lectures on Buddhist Literature in China* (London, 1882, p. 8) Beal says that the Dhammapada was translated in China between A. D. 149 and 171. But he did not know whether this version was extant.

[14] Of these thirty-nine chapters, Nos. g to 32, and 34 and 35, agree in titles with the twenty-six chapters of the Pâli, and in the same order. Beal assures us that not only the titles, but the text is identical in that early Chinese version, except for some additions. Chapters 7, 8, 16 and 19, however, contain the same number of stanzas as the Chinese; while most of the rest are added to, the number of extra stanzas ranging from one only in Chapters 3 and 4, to twelve in Chapter 17. Chapters 18 and 21 have two verses less in the Chinese, and Chapter 26 one less. It is to be regretted that Beal chose the Parable Recension for translation instead of the earlier and truer version, and thereby brought forth the disparaging comparison made by Rhys Davids, in his Hibbert Lectures, between that recension and the Pâli. Let us hope that Teitaro Suzuki will give us the earliest Chinese version obtainable, whether that of the third century or that of the second.

I. Antitheses

1. Creatures from mind their character derive,
     Mind-marshaled are they, and mind-made:
     If with a mind corrupt one speak or act,
     Him doth pain follow,
     As the wheel the beast of burden's foot.

2. Creatures from mind their character derive,
     Mind-marshaled are they, and mind-made:
     If with pure mind one speak or act,
     Him doth happiness follow,
     Even as a shadow that declineth not.

3. "He abused me, beat me,
        Overcame me, robbed me!"
     Those with such thoughts imbued
     Have not their anger calmed.

4. "He abused me, beat me,
        Overcame me, robbed me!"
     Those not with such thoughts imbued
     Have their anger calmed.

5. Not indeed by anger
        Are angers here calmed ever:
     By meekness are they calmed.
     This is an ancient doctrine.

6. The many know not
        That we here must end;
     But those who know it
     Have their quarrels calmed.

7. The man who dwelleth contemplating pleasure,
        With faculties incontinent,
     In food immoderate,
     Slothful, weak of will,
     Him surely Mâro overthrows,
     As wind a weakling tree.

8. The man who dwelleth unregarding pleasure,
   With faculties thoroughly continent,
   In food moderate, having faith, of strenuous will
   Him Mâro no more overthroweth
   Than wind a stony mount.

9. He who, from Depravities not free,
   Would don the yellow garb,
   Void of temperance and truth,
   Is not worthy of the yellow.

10. But he who hath spewed out Depravities,
    And is well grounded in morals,
    With temperance and truth endowed,
    He indeed is worthy of the yellow.

11. Those who imagine the essential in the nonessential.
    And see the non-essential in the essential,
    They arrive not at the essential;
    They are in the realm of false resolve.

12. But those who know the essential and the non essential
    To be what they are,
    They at the essential do arrive;
    They are in the realm of Right Resolve.

13. Even as rain
    An ill-thatched house doth penetrate,
    So penetrateth passion
    An heart ill-trained in thought.

14. Even as rain doth penetrate not
    A well-thatched house,
    So passion penetrateth not
    An heart well-trained in thought.

15. He sorroweth here,
    He sorroweth hereafter;
    Bothwise doth sorrow the evil doer:
    He sorroweth, he mourneth,
    When he seeth his own deed's foulness.

16. He rejoiceth here,
    He rejoiceth hereafter,
    Bothwise rejoiceth the doer of good:
    He rejoiceth, he doubly rejoiceth,
    When he seeth his own deed's clarity.

17. He is tortured here,
    He is tortured hereafter,
    Bothwise is tortured the evil doer;
    He is tortured by the thought:
    "'Twas I who did that wrong!"
    Still more is he tortured,
    When to perdition gone.

18. Here is he glad, hereafter glad,
    The doer of good is bothwise glad;
    He is glad at the thought:
    "'Twas I who did that good!"
    Still more is he glad
    When gone to Bliss.

19. Should one recite a portion large,
    Yet not a worker be, but a careless man,
    He is like a cowherd counting others' kine,
    And hath no part in the philosophic life.

20. Should one recite a little portion of Doctrine,
    But lead a life according thereunto,
    Renouncing passion, hate, stupidity,
    Truly knowing, with heart set truly free,
    Caring for naught here or hereafter,
    He hath a part in the philosophic life.

NOTES TO CHAPTER I.

1, 2. The word "creatures" translates the Pâli *dhammâ* which in its full significance has no equivalent in English. In the singular (dhammo, Sanskrit, dharmas), it means law, truth, religion, doctrine; and as an adjective "spiritual" as opposed to carnal. It is derived from the root *Dhar*, and is etymologically connected with the Latin *forma* and the English *form*, denoting the form of things, and the law that determines their being. In this latter sense, Fausböll renders the plural *dhammâ* in Latin by *naturae*, viz., things, creatures, beings, types of being, the nature or character of existences.

The opening lines of the first and second stanzas mean: "All things (viz., the various types of all objects, among them especially living beings) derive from mind the principle that determines their character and rules their nature." Fausböll translates it: *Naturae a mente principium ducunt.*

The Japanese commentator explains the sentence by stating that things have "Kokorowo shuto shite," i.e., "mind as if it were their master." The Chinese translator renders the term *manas* by *hsin*, "the kernel of things," which otherwise means "heart, soul, mind, intellect, etc."

Dr. Carus is responsible for this note in the main, and also for the rendering of the first line and a half.

7. Mâro, the Buddhist Tempter, is not purely evil, like the Zoroastrian and Christian Devil, but an angel in good standing; being the ruler of the highest sphere of *devas*, immediately below the seraphic *brahmâ-heaven*. Karl Neumann considers him the equivalent of the Greek Pan.

19, 20. These allusions to the systematic recitation of the sacred lore are important. Some monks were required to learn more others less. See Max Müller's note here, and Stanzas 363-366 below.

II. Earnestness

21. Earnestness is the immortal path,
    Carelessness the path of death;
    The earnest do not die;
    'Tis the careless who are like unto the dead.

22. Those who know this distinctly,
    Pandits in earnestness,
    Rejoice in earnestness,
    Delighting in the lot of the elect.

23. These meditative ones, persevering,
    Ever strong and valiant,
    Being wise, attain Nirvâna,
    Yoga-calm supreme.

24. The glory groweth
    Of one who is aroused and recollecting,
    Clean of deed, considerate in his doing,
    Restrained, righteous in life, and earnest.

25. By rousing himself, by earnestness,
    Restraint and temperance,
    Let the wise man make himself an island
    Which no flood can overwhelm.

26. Unto carelessness are yoked the fools,
    The fellows who have no wisdom;
    But the wise man guardeth earnestness
    As a financier his wealth.

27. Let none to carelessness be yoked,
    To love's delight and intimacy,
    For the earnest, meditative man
    Obtains an ample joy.

28. When the pandit putteth away
    Carelessness by earnestness,
    Ascending unsorrowing
    To the palace-roof of intellect,
    That wise one looketh on a sorrowing race,
    Yea, upon fools,
    Even as a mountaineer upon a groundling.

29. Earnest among the careless,
    Among sleepers wide awake,
    The wise man goeth on his way,
    Like a swift horse leaving the laggard behind.

30. By earnestness did Indra get
    The lordship of the gods:
    Men praise the earnest man;
    The careless is ever despised.

31. A monk delighting in earnestness,
    Or of carelessness afraid,
    Burning every fetter, be it minute or big,
    Goeth about as fire.

32. A monk delighting in earnestness,
    Or of carelessness afraid,
    Is not liable to be lost,
    Unto Nirvâna nigh.

NOTES TO CHAPTER II.

26. I translate the last line according to the Prâkrit fragment from Chinese Turkestan. This is a case where an ancient version can correct corruption of the text.

III. The Heart

33. His trembling, fluctuating heart,
     So hard to guard, so hard to hold in check,
     The wise man maketh straight,
     As a fletcher an arrow.

34. Like a being born of water
     And thrown upon dry land,
     Taken from house and home,
     This heart doth flutter
     To renounce the Tempter's realm.

35. Hard to hold in, the heart,
     Flighty, alighting where it listeth;
     Good the taming thereof:
     The tamed heart bringeth ease.

36. Hard to perceive indeed,
     So artful is the heart, alighting where it listeth;
     Let the wise man guard it:
     The guarded heart bringeth ease.

37. Far-faring, lone-going,
     Bodiless, lying in the cave,
     Is the heart; and they that bridle it
     Shall be delivered from the Tempter's bonds.

38. The intellect of the wayward-hearted one
     Who knoweth not the Gospel,
     Whose calm is troubled,
     Grows not to the full.

39. To him whose heart runs not away,
     Whose thought is not perplexed,
     Who hath renounced both merit and demerit:
     Unto him, the watchful, there is no fear.

40. Knowing that this body is like a potter's vessel,
     Stablishing this heart like a fort,
     Subjugate the Tempter with the sword of intellect;
     And when he is conquered, guard him,
     And be without abode.

41. Ere long, alas! this body
    On the earth will lie,
    Despised, of consciousness bereft,
    E'en as a useless log.

42. Whate'er a foeman to a foe may do—
    The wrathful to the wrathful—
    The ill-directed heart can do it worse.

43. What neither mother nor father,
    Nor other kinsfolk can do
    A rightly directed heart
    Can do better.

NOTES TO CHAPTER III.

Chapter III., Title. *Citta* is the emotional mind, i. e. "the heart." (Rhys Davids.) Cf. the New Testament διανοία.

37. *Sutta-Nipâto* 772 makes "the cave" mean the body. (Fausböll.)

38. The term "gospel" (*saddhammo*) is a genuinely Buddhist conception. See Glossary.

IV. Flowers

44. Who shall conquer this earth
    And Hades and the angel-world?
    Who shall cull the well-taught Dhammapada,
    Even as an expert a flower?

45. A disciple shall conquer the earth
    And Hades and the angel-world;
    A disciple shall cull the well-taught Dhammapada,
    Even as an expert a flower.

46. Knowing this body to be like foam,
    Supremely understanding its nature of mirage,
    Breaking the flower-pointed [arrows] of the Tempter,
    Let him arrive at non-vision of Death's king.

47. A man who culleth flowers
    With mind distraught
    Doth Death bear off
    As a flood the sleeping village.

48. A man who culleth flowers
    With mind distraught
    The Ender subjugates
    While yet with lusts unsatisfied.

49. As the bee, hurting not the flower,
    Its color or its fragrance,
    Flieth away with the nectar,
    So let a sage live in a village.

50. Not others' ways perverse,
    Not others' done or undone deed,
    But his own deeds
    Done and undone must he regard.

51. Like the delightsome flower,
    Splendid but scentless,
    Is the fine-said fruitless word
    Of him that doeth not.

52. Like the delightsome flower,
 Splendid and fragrant,
 Is the fine-said fruitful word
 Of him that doeth.

53. As from an heap of flowers
 Can garlands manifold be made,
 So by a mortal, when he once is born,
 Much goodness can be done.

54. Neither against the wind
 The scent of flowers
 Goeth, nor sandal fragrance,
 Jasmine, nor rose-bay;
 But the odor of the genuine
 Doth go against the wind:
 A good soul pervadeth every clime.

55. Sandal-wood, rose-bay,
 Lotus and aloes:
 Far beyond these natural scents
 Is the odor of virtue.

56. Mean is this scent,
 Which is rose-bay and sandal-wood;
 But the odor of the righteous is superb,
 And is wafted to the gods.

57. The Tempter findeth not the way of those
 Endowed with virtue, living earnestly,
 Emancipated by thorough knowledge.

58. Even as on a rubbish-heap
 Thrown upon the highway,
 A lily there may grow,
 Sweet-scented, fine:—

59. So among the rubbish of beings,
 Among the blinded vulgar,
 The disciple of the fully Enlightened One
 Outshineth [all] by intellect.

NOTE TO CHAPTER IV.

44, 45. Max Müller translates *Dhammapada* as "path of virtue," while Hû has "les vers de la Loi." I leave it untranslated: it is the title of our present hymn-book, and is charged with many meanings. See verse 102.

V. Fools

60. Long the night unto the wakeful,
    Long the league unto the weary;
    Long to fools is transmigration,
    To those who wot not of the Gospel.

61. If the traveler meet not
    With his better or his equal,
    Let him make his lonely journey strong:
    With a fool there is no fellowship.

62. "These sons are mine, this wealth is mine,"
    The fool torments himself to think,
    When he himself is not his own:
    Much less the sons, much less the wealth.

63. The fool who knows he is a fool,
    A pandit is at least in this;
    But the fool who thinks himself a pandit,
    He is called a fool indeed.

64. Should a fool wait upon a scholar all his life,
    He knoweth the Doctrine no more
    Than a spoon the taste of soup.

65. Should a wise man wait upon a scholar
    Even for a moment,
    He quickly knoweth the Doctrine,
    As the tongue the taste of soup.

66. Fools walk unreflecting,
    With themselves for enemies,
    Doing an evil deed which hath bitter fruit.

67. Not well done is that deed
    Which, done, torments a man;
    The reward whereof he receiveth
    Weeping, with tearful face.

68. But that deed is well done
    Which, done, tormenteth not:
    The reward whereof he receiveth
    Gladly and with joy.

69. So long as evil ripeneth not,
    The fool thinketh it honey;
    But when ripeneth the evil,
    Then suffereth he pain.

70. Month after month the fool
    May feed on food ascetic-wise,
    But he is not worth a tithe
    Of those who weigh the Doctrine.

71. The evil deed when done
    Is like new-drawn milk which turns not:
    It followeth the burning fool,
    Like fire concealed in ashes.

72. And when, revealed at last,
    'Tis born for mischief to the fool,
    His fortune it destroyeth,
    And cleaveth his head.

73. Unjust repute he may desire,
    Precedence among monks,
    Lordship in the monasteries,
    And honors in strange families.

74. "Let householders and hermits both
    Deem that I do whate'er is done,
    To me alone let them be subject in everything,
    And in deeds to be done or not."
    Such is a fool's imagination;
    Desire groweth, and eke pride.

75. "One is the way that leadeth unto gain;
    Another the way that goeth to Nirvâna":
    Supremely understanding this,
    A monk who is Buddha's disciple
    Should not rejoice in honor,
    But cultivate seclusion.

NOTE TO CHAPTER V.

70. "Ascetic-wise," literally "with a grass-point." "Tithe" is literally "sixteenth part," but this is for metrical effect in the Pâli.

VI. The Pandit (*or, Scholar*)

76. Should one see a revealer of treasures,
    Who showeth what to shun,
    Reproving, wise,
    Then such a pandit let him cultivate.
    'Tis better, not worse,
    For him that cultivateth such.

77. Let him exhort, instruct, deter from wrong:
    Dear is he to the genuine, but hateful to the false.

78. Take not for friends the wicked,
    Take not the lowest men;
    Cultivate friends who are good,
    Cultivate the best of men.

79. Drinker of Doctrine, with heart serene,
    Peaceful in his lying down,
    The pandit rejoiceth ever
    In the Doctrine made known by the Elect.

80. Pipe-makers lead the water,
    And fletchers carve the dart,
    Carpenters carve the wood,
    And pandits tame themselves.

81. Even as a solid block of rock
    Is not shaken by the wind,
    So pandits falter not mid blame or praise.

82. E'en as a lake, deep, still and clear,
    Pandits are still when listening to the laws.

83. The good go on, whate'er befall,
    The genuine prattle not in lust and lusts;
    When touched by weal or woe
    Pandits appear no different.

84. Not for his own or others' sake
    Son, wealth or kingdom one should wish;
    He should not by injustice wish his own success,
    But be moral, intelligent and just.

85. Few among men the mortals
    Who arrive at yonder shore:
    The rest of the race run hither and thither along the bank.

86. Those who follow the Doctrine
    When the Doctrine is rightly preached
    Are the mortals who will pass beyond
    The realm of Death, so hard to cross.

87. Leaving the black doctrine,
    Let a pandit study the white,
    Going from home to homelessness,
    Where in seclusion delights are few.

88. Let him desire delight supernal there,
    Forsaking lusts, possessing naught;
    Let the pandit purge himself
    From troubles of the heart.

89. They whose hearts are thoroughly well trained
    In the Articles of Full Enlightenment,
    Who cling to naught and rejoice when fancy-free;
    Who have destroyed Depravities and are full of light,—
    Have [even] in the world attained Nirvâna.

NOTES TO CHAPTER VI.

87. Or: Leaving the dark state,
    Let a pandit embrace the bright.

89. "Articles," literally "members." In the *Book of the Great Decease*, they are called, in the translation, "the seven kinds of wisdom."

VII. The Arahat

90. His journey done, the griefless one,
    On every hand set free,
    All bonds renounced, no suffering knows.

91. The thoughtful struggle onward,
    And delight not in abode:
    Like swans who leave a lake,
    Do they leave house and home.

92. For whom there is no store of wealth,
    Who live on food prescribed,
    The sphere of whom is freedom
    Void and imageless,—Of such the course is hard to
    follow,
    Like that of birds in air.

93. He whose Depravities are destroyed,
    Who liveth not by bread alone,
    The sphere of whom is freedom
    Void and imageless,—
    Of him the path is hard to follow,
    Like that of birds in air.

94. Him whose faculties have come to calm,
    Like horses well tamed by a charioteer,—
    His pride renounced,
    Depravities destroyed,—
    Such a man the very gods do envy.

95. Like the earth, he doth not quarrel;
    Such a dutiful one is like the threshold-stone,
    Or a lake that hath no mud:
    Transmigrations are not for such.

96. Quiet his mind is,
    Quiet the speech and deed
    Of such, by thorough knowledge
    Emancipated, calmed.

97. The man who is not credulous,
    Knowing the non-made, cutting off intercourse,
    Deprived of access, spewing out desire:
    He indeed is the highest soul.

98. Whether in village or in forest,
    On ocean or on shore,
    Wherever Arahats abide,
    That spot delightsome is.

99. Delightful are the woods,
    Wherein a worldling delighteth not.
    The passionless will find delight:
    They hunt not lust.

NOTES TO CHAPTER VII.

93. "Who liveth not by bread alone." Literally, "independent of food." "Food" here is a metaphysical term.

97. "Access" is also rendered "occasion," "opportunity," and may mean opportunity for temptation.

VIII. Thousands

100. If a speech be a thousand words,
    Of senseless sentences composed,
    Better is one sensible sentence,
    Which bringeth calm when heard.

101. If a poem be a thousands words,
    Of senseless lines composed,
    Better is a poem of one line,
    Which bringeth calm when heard.

102. Should one recite an hundred poems,
    Of senseless lines composed,
    Better is one Line of the Doctrine (*one Dhammapada*),
    Which bringeth calm when heard.

103. He who a thousand thousand men
    Should conquer in the fight,
    And then should conquer himself alone,
    The prince of fighters he.

104. Better 'tis oneself to conquer
    Than all the race beside:
    Unto the man self-tamed,
    Ever restrained in living,—

105. Neither angel nor genius, Tempter nor God,
    Can unto such a mortal
    Make victory defeat.

106. Should one sacrifice with a thousand
    Each month for an hundred years,
    And then worship
    For one moment the self-cultured,
    Better that worship
    Than a century of sacrifice.

107. Should a man for a century
    Tend in the forest the [sacred] fire,
    And then worship
    For one moment the self-cultured,
    Better that worship
    Than a century of sacrifice.

108. Whatever oblation or sacrifice in the world
     A man may sacrifice for a year, expecting reward,—
     All that is not worth a farthing:
     Better is reverence for the righteous.

109. To one whose wont is reverent greeting ever,
     Honoring the aged,
     Four things increase:
     Life, beauty, happiness and power.

110. If one should live an hundred years,
     Immoral, discomposed,
     Better to him were life one day
     When virtuous and enrapt.

111. If one should live an hundred years,
     Ignorant, discomposed,
     Better to him were life one day
     Intelligent, enrapt.

112. If one should live an hundred years
     Inert and weak of will,
     Better to him were life one day,
     Exerting will-power strong.

113. If one should live an hundred years
     Not seeing origin and end,
     Better to him were life one day,
     When seeing origin and end.

114. If one should live an hundred years
     Not seeing the immortal path,
     Better to him were life one day,
     When seeing the immortal path.

115. If one should live an hundred years
     Not seeing the highest Doctrine,
     Better to him were life one day
     When seeing the highest Doctrine.

NOTES TO CHAPTER VIII.

100, 101. "Sentence" and "line" represent the same word, *pada*, literally "foot."

106, 107. The language is ambiguous, and may mean either that he is to worship his solitary self (Fausböll) or the self-trained sage (Max Müller and Hû). By analogy with 103, it would seem to be the former: *ekan* then qualifies "self" instead of "moment."

109. This verse is in the Law-Book of Manu.

IX. Evil (*or Wrong*)

116. Let one hasten unto goodness,
     And from evil keep his heart:
     If one do right perfunctorily,
     His mind delights in wrong.

117. If a man do wrong,
     Let him not do it repeatedly;
     Let him not take pleasure therein:
     Painful is wrong's accumulation.

118. If a man do right,
     Let him do it again and again;
     Let him take pleasure therein:
     Happiness is an accumulation of right.

119. Even an evil man seeth good
     So long as evil ripeneth not;
     But when ripeneth the evil,
     Then seeth he evil things.

120. Even a good man seeth evil,
     So long as goodness ripeneth not;
     But when ripeneth the goodness,
     Then good things doth he see.

121. Let no one think lightly of evil, saying:
     "'Twill not come nigh to me":
     By drops of water falling
     Is the water-pitcher filled;
     The fool is filled with evil,
     Though little by little he gather it.

122. Let no one think lightly of good, saying:
     "'Twill not come nigh to me":
     By drops of water falling
     Is the water-pitcher filled;
     The sage is filled with goodness,
     Though little by little he gather it.

123. Shun evils
　　As a life-lover the poison,
　　Or as a merchant, with much wealth and few companions,
　　The dangerous road.

124. If on the hand there be no wound,
　　Then in his hand may one take poison;
　　Poison affecteth not the unwounded:
　　There is no evil unto him who doeth it not.

125. Should one offend an innocent man,
　　A pure and blameless person,
　　Only upon that fool recoils the wrong,
　　Even as light dust thrown against the wind.

126. Some to a womb are born again;
　　Wrong-doers unto hell;
　　To Paradise the pious go;
　　The sinless to Nirvâna.

127. Not in the sky
　　Nor in the midst of the sea,
　　Nor entering a cleft of the mountains,
　　Is found that realm on earth
　　Where one may stand and be
　　From an evil deed absolved.

128. Not in the sky
　　Nor in the midst of the sea,
　　Nor entering a cleft of the mountains,
　　Is found that realm on earth,
　　Where one may stand
　　And death subdue him not.

NOTES TO CHAPTER IX.

117. Owing to the Pâli use of nouns and adjectives interchangeably, this may also be translated:
"Pain is an accumulation of wrong."

126. "Paradise," the *Swarga* of popular Hindû belief. "Sinless" is literally, "without the Depravities" (*âsavâ*).

X. The Rod

129. At the rod do all men tremble,
     And death do all men fear:
     Putting oneself in their place,
     Kill not nor cause to kill.

130. At the rod do all men tremble;
     Unto all men life is dear:
     Do as you would be done by;
     Kill not nor cause to kill.

131. He who with the rod doth hurt
     Beings that long for happiness,
     Wishing for happiness himself,
     Findeth not happiness after death.

132. He who doth hurt not with the rod
     Beings that long for happiness,
     Wishing for happiness himself,
     He findeth happiness after death.

133. Speak not harshly to any one:
     Those spoken to might answer thee.
     Painful indeed is language violent:
     Revenges might pursue thee.

134. Shouldst thou from utterance keep thyself,
     Like to a broken gong,
     Then hast thou reached Nirvâna:
     With thee is found no violence.

135. Even as a cowherd driveth kine
     To pasture with a rod,
     So do old age and death
     Drive the life of the living.

136. Doing his evil deeds
     The fool is not awake;
     The stupid man is tortured by his deeds
     As one is burnt with fire.

137. Whoso with rod among the rodless
     To the harmless doeth harm,
     Quickly to one of these ten states doth come:

138. A cruel suffering shall he meet,
     A loss, his body's breach,
     A heavy sickness, or distracted mind;

139. Or else misfortune from a king,
     An accusation terrible,
     Kinsfolk's mortality or loss of wealth;

140. Or lightning-fire his houses burns,
     And at the body's wreck
     The fool is born to hell.

141. Not the practice of nakedness,
     Nor matted hair, nor dirt,
     Not fasting or lying on the ground,
     Not rubbing with dust
     Or sitting motionless,
     Can purify a mortal
     Who hath not transcended doubt.

142. E'en though adorned,
     If one should walk in peace,
     Peaceful, subdued, restrained and chaste,—
     The rod among all beings laid aside,—
     He is the brahmin, the philosopher, the monk.

143. Is there in the world
     Found any man by shame withheld
     Who averteth censure
     As a good horse the whip?
     Even as a good horse
     In contact with the whip,]
     Be ye ardent and swift.

144. By faith, by morals, and by power of will,
     By trance, by discrimination of doctrine,
     Endowed with wisdom in conduct, and mentally
         collected,
     Ye shall renounce this pain, which is no small one.

145. Pipe-makers lead the water,
And fletchers carve the dart,
Carpenters carve the wood,
And good men tame themselves.

NOTES TO CHAPTER X.

129, 130. "Putting oneself in their place," and, "Do as you would be done by," are two variant translations of the same words, literally: "Having made oneself a likeness." This is the Hindû form of the GOLDEN RULE.

133. "Revenges" is literally *return-rods*; hence its appositeness in this chapter. *Rod* in prose means punishment, but in poetry the literal term is better.

138. Here *citta* is rendered "mind." Following Rhys Davids, I usually render it by "heart."

XI. Old Age

146. What laughter now, what joy
     In being always on fire?
     In darkness wrapped, ye will not seek a light.

147. Behold [this] variegated figure,
     [This] congested body of wounds;
     Ailing, with many a resolve,
     It hath not firmness or stability.

148. Wasted this form, a nest of disease, and frail;
     Broken the mass of foulness,
     For life at the end is death.

149. What are these things like gourds
     In autumn tossed away?
     White bones: when seen, what delight?

150. Of bones is made the citadel,
     With mortar of flesh and blood,
     Wherein are stowed away old age,
     Death, pride and hypocrisy!

151. Wax old the gaudy chariots of kings,
     The body also doth approach old age;
     But the nature of the genuine approacheth not old age:
     Thus do the genuine to the genuine say.

152. This man of little learning
     Waxeth old, like an ox;
     His fleshly parts do grow,
     But his intellect groweth not.

153. Many a life to transmigrate,
     Long quest, no rest, hath been my fate,
     Tent-designer inquisitive for:
     Painful birth from state to state.

154. Tent-designer! I know thee now;
     Never again to build art thou:
     Quite out are all thy joyful fires,
     Rafter broken and roof-tree gone;
     Into the Vast my heart goes on,
     Gains Eternity—dead desires.

155. Those who have been unchaste,
     And gotten not wealth in youth,
     Like old herons, are consumed,
     As in a pond devoid of fish.

156. Those who have lived not the religious life,
     And gotten not wealth in youth,
     Lie like worn-out bows,
     Bewailing the olden [times.]

NOTES TO CHAPTER XI.

153, 154 These verses are the Hymn of Victory sung by Buddha when he reached Enlightenment under the Bo-Tree, and they constitute the primal words of Buddhist Holy Writ. I have departed here from my usual method, and given a freer rendering, so as to convey some remote echo of the melody of the Pâli. In verse 154, the *word phâsukâ* is a pun, meaning both "rafters" and "pleasures." The literal meaning is as follows:

> Manifold-birth-transmigration
> Have I run through, not finding
> House-maker seeking:
> Painful birth again-again.

> O house-maker! seen art thou,
> Again [a] house not shalt thou make:
> All thy rafters broken, house-peak destroyed;
> Dissolution[15] gone heart, of[16] thirsts destruction has reached.

By permission of Professor Charles R. Lanman, of Harvard University, we give his rendering as follows:—

---

[15] Lit. apart from Samkhârâ.
[16] Gen. pl.

Thro' birth and rebirth's endless round
I ran and sought, but never found
Who framed and built this house of clay.
What misery!—birth for ay and ay!

O builder! thee at last I see!
Ne'er shalt thou build again for me.

Thy rafters all are broken now,
Demolished lies thy ridge-pole, low.

My heart, demolished too, I ween,
An end of all desire hath seen.

For Rhys Davids's translation, see his *Buddhist Birth-Stories.*
Warren has one also in his *Buddhism in Translations*, p. 83.

155, 156. The first line in each is identical. Variant translations are given of the ambiguous word *brahmacaryam*, which means both "religious life" and "chastity.".

XII. Oneself

157. Himself if one hold dear,
     With good guard should he guard him:
     Of three night watches, during one
     The scholar should keep vigil.

158. Himself should one first establish in the right,
     Then should he teach another:
     The scholar should not be disgraced.

159. Himself if one would make
     Suchwise as he teacheth another,
     Well tamed, let him make [others] tame.
     Alas! 'Tis said oneself is hard to tame.

160. Ah! Self is master of self:
     Who else could master be?
     Yea, by a self well tamed
     One getteth a master hard to get.

161. By self alone is evil done,
     Self-born it is, self-bred;
     It grindeth the fool to powder,
     As a diamond the flinty gem.

162. He who is exceedingly immoral,
     Like a sâl-tree which a creeper overgrows,
     Maketh himself such
     As his enemy wisheth him.

163. Easily done are things not good,
     Unhealthful to oneself;
     But what is healthful and good,
     That indeed is hard in the highest to do.

164. The fool who scorneth the religion of the Arahats,
     Of the right-living Elect,
     Inclining unto speculation false,
     Ripeneth unto self-destruction,
     Like the fruits of the rosea-reed.

165. By self alone is evil done,
    By self is one disgraced;
    By self is evil left undone,
    By self alone is he purified;
    Purity and impurity belong to self:
    No one can purify another.

166. His own duty for another's,
    How great soe'er, let none neglect;
    His own duty, when he hath supernally known,
    Unto that duty let him be applied.

NOTES TO CHAPTER XII.

157. Compare Mark xiii. 37.

161. Compare Luke xx. 18, which has been copied by scribes into Matthew, where it does not belong. (Matth. xxi. 44.) I have shown, in an unpublished work, that Luke abounds more in Buddhist parallels than the other Evangelists.

165. Compare *Sutta Nipâto* 906.

XIII. The World

167. A base religion follow not,
     Live not in carelessness;
     False speculation follow not,
     Be not a world-supporter.

168. Rise up, be not careless,
     Walk in the virtuous religion;
     He who walketh in religion resteth in peace
     In this world and the next.

169. Walk in the virtuous religion,
     Walk not in the immoral one;
     He who walketh in religion resteth in peace
     In this world and the next.

170. See it as a bubble, see it as mirage:
     The King of Death seeth not him
     Who thus looketh on the world.

171. Come, see this world, glittering
     Like to a kingly chariot,
     Wherein fools are plunged.
     But for the wise there is no tie.

172. He who was careless once
     And afterwards was not so,
     Doth illuminate this world,
     As the moon set free from cloud.

173. He whose evil deed is covered by a good one
     Doth illuminate this world,
     As the moon set free from cloud.

174. Dark is this world, few see clearly here;
     Few, as birds from the net escaped,
     Go unto Paradise.

175. Swans on the path of the sun go forth,
     They go in the air by miracle:
     The wise are led from the world away,
     Having foiled the Tempter and all his train.

176. For a man who transgresseth a single law,
And lieth and scoffs at another world,
There is no evil he cannot do.

177. The niggard go not to the angel-world;
'Tis fools who praise not liberality,
But the wise man rejoiceth in a gift:
By that alone is he happy in the life beyond.

178. Better than empire over earth,
Better than going to Paradise,
Better than lordship over all the worlds,
Is the fruit of entering the Path.

NOTES TO CHAPTER XIII.

169. While Buddha maintained that only his own religion could take men to Nirvâna, yet he was tolerant toward others, provided they laid stress upon ethics. See Numerical Collection VII. 62, translated by me in *The Open Court* (Chicago) for July, 1901. Here we are told that a former religion had taken men to heaven and to God, but not to Nirvâna. In the Middling Collection, Dialogue No. 71, Gotamo says that naked ascetics rarely go to paradise because of their neglect of ethics. Other Scriptures affirm that only Buddhists are assured of final release. At the same time Buddhism has always been tolerant, and when it enjoyed political power did not persecute other faiths, but only heresies of its own.

177. "Liberality" and "gift" are the same word: *dânam.*

XIV. The Buddha

179. One there is whose conquest is reconquered not,
Whose conquest no one in the world can win:
The Buddha, infinite in sphere
And pathless. Him by what path will ye lead?

180. One there is whom no ensnaring poisonous desire can
lead astray:
The Buddha, infinite in sphere
And pathless. Him by what path will ye lead?

181. The wise, on trance intent,
Glad with renunciation's calm,
Those real Buddhas, with collected minds,
The very gods do envy.

182. Hard is the conception of a man,
Hard is the life of mortals,
Hard the hearing of the Gospel,
Hard the arising of the Buddhas.

183. Ceasing to do all wrong,
Initiation into goodness,
Cleansing the heart:
This is the religion of the Buddhas.

184. Patience and long-suffering
Are the supreme asceticism—
Supreme Nirvâna, say the Buddhas;
For he is not an hermit who hurteth another,
Not a philosopher who annoyeth another.

185. Meekness, non-resistance,
Restraint under the Confessional,
Temperance in eating, secluded residence,
And devotion to high thought:
This is the religion of the Buddhas.

186. Not by a rain of guineas
Could lusts be satisfied.
Little sweetness, [long] pain: such are lusts.
Knowing this, is one a pandit.

187. Even in lusts divine
    He findeth no delight:
    Delighted in Thirst's destruction
    Is the disciple of the real Buddha.

188. To many a refuge do they go—
    To [holy] mounts and groves;
    To temple gardens and memorial trees—
    Men driven on by dread.

189. Such refuge is not sure,
    Such refuge is not final;
    Not to such refuge going
    Is one from every pain released.

190. Behold him who unto the Buddha,
    Unto the Doctrine, unto the Order
    For a refuge goeth,
    And with clear intellect doth see
    Four Noble Truths:

191. Pain and Pain's Origin
    And Pain's Demise,
    Yea, and the Noble Eightfold Way
    That leadeth to the quieting of Pain:

192. There is the refuge sure,
    There is the refuge final:
    Unto such refuge going
    From every pain is one released.

193. Hard to find is an high-born soul,
    Not everywhere can such be born:
    Where that wise man is born
    In bliss doth thrive the family.

194. Blessed is the arising of the Buddhas,
    Blessed the preaching of the Gospel,
    Blessed the concord of the Order,
    Blest the devotion of concordant men.

195. For him who worshippeth the worshipful,
    Be they Buddhas or disciples,
    Who have transcended phenomena,
    Crossed the [current of] sorrows and laments,—

196. For him who worshippeth such
    As are in Nirvâna, beyond the reach of fear,
    No one his mighty merit e'er can measure.
    Here endeth the First Lection (or, Recital).

NOTES TO CHAPTER XIV.

180. "Poisonous" represents an ambiguity, which may mean "widespread."

181. Disciples, as well as the Masters, are called Buddha (Enlightened), as in Long Collection, Dialogue No. 23, where the term is applied to Kumârakassapo.

XV. Happiness

197. Ah! Live we happily in sooth,
     Unangered 'mid the angry;
     'Mid angry men let us unangered live.

198. Ah! Live we happily in sooth,
     Unailing 'mid the ailing;
     'Mid ailing men let us unailing live.

199. Ah! Live we happily in sooth,
     Without greed among the greedy;
     'Mid greedy men let us live free from greed.

200. Ah! Live we happily in sooth,—
     We who have nothing:
     Feeders on joy shall we be,
     Even as the Angels of Splendor.

201. Victory breedeth anger,
     For in pain the vanquished lieth:
     Lieth happy the man of peace,
     Renouncing victory and defeat.

202. There is no fire like passion,
     No evil luck like hate,
     No pain compared to finite elements,
     No happiness higher than peace.

203. Hunger the supreme disease,
     Existence the supremest pain:
     To know that this is really so
     Is Nirvâna, happiness supreme.

204. The greatest gain is health,
     The greatest wealth content,
     Confidence is the best of kin,
     Nirvâna happiness supreme.

205. When he drinketh the juice of seclusion
     And the juice of quietude,
     Painless is one, and guileless,
     Drinking the juice of joy in the Doctrine.

206. Good is the sight of the Elect;
Living with them is happiness ever;
By not seeing fools
May man be lastingly happy.

207. Walking in company with fools
One suffereth all his life:
Painful the society of fools,
As if with an enemy ever;
But happy the society of the wise,
Like meeting with kinsfolk.

208. Therefore 'tis true:
The wise, intelligent and learned man,
Patient, devout, elect,
That upright soul, distinguished, follow ye,
As the moon the starry path.

NOTES TO CHAPTER XV.

200. The angels of Splendor are a celestial order who are unaffected by the dissolution of the universe when the abodes of lower orders are destroyed.

202. "Finite elements," Pâli *khandhâ*; Sanskrit *skandhâs*

203. "Existence," *Samkhârâ*, constituents of existence.

XVI. Pleasure

209. He who by distraction is attracted,
     And by abstraction is attracted not,
     Renouncing reality, grabbing at pleasure,
     Envieth the self-abstracted.

210. Seek not ever for things pleasant or unpleasant:
     Not seeing pleasant things is pain,
     And seeing the unpleasant is.

211. Therefore make nothing dear:
     The loss of the endeared is evil;
     Bonds are unknown to those
     For whom there is naught dear or otherwise.

212. From endearment sorrow is born,
     From endearment fear is born:
     For him who from endearment is delivered
     Sorrow is not, much less fear.

213. Sorrow is born from love,
     And fear from love is born:
     For him who is emancipated from love,
     Sorrow is not, nor fear.

214. From delight is sorrow born,
     And fear from delight is born:
     For one delivered from delight,
     Sorrow is not, nor fear.

215. Sorrow is born from lust,
     And fear from lust is born:
     For one from lust delivered,
     Sorrow is not, nor fear.

216. From Thirst is sorrow born,
     And fear is born from Thirst:
     For one from Thirst set free,
     Sorrow is not, nor fear.

217. With virtue and insight endued,
     Righteous, truth-telling,
     Minding his own affairs,
     Him do the common folk hold dear.

218. When springs the wish for the Ineffable,
     Then may one thrill with mind;
     And when in lusts the heart is not bound down,
     "Carried-up-stream" the man is called.

219. A man long absent,
     Safe from afar returned,
     Do kinsfolk, friends, familiars
     Welcome returned.

220. E'en so good deeds
     Receive the doer thereof,
     When gone from this world to the next,
     Just as the kinsfolk the dear one returned.

NOTES TO CHAPTER XVI.

209. "Abstraction," *yogo.* I have tried to preserve the paronomasia here.

211. "Dear" and "pleasant" are the same word (*piyo*).

XVII. Anger

221. Anger renounce, relinquish pride,
Pass beyond every fetter:
Him who to Name and Form doth cling not,
Him who possesseth nothing,
Pains never overtake.

222. He who his risen anger holdeth,
Like to a rolling chariot,
Him do I call a charioteer:
Other folk hold the reins.

223. Overcome anger with kindness,
Overcome evil with good,
Overcome meanness with a gift,
Ay, and a liar with truth.

224. Speak the truth, be not angry,
Give when asked for a little:
By these points a man may go
Into the presence of the gods.

225. Sages who injure none,
Restrained in body ever,
Go to the changeless place,
Where gone they mourn no more.

226. For those who ever watch,
And study night and day,
Aspiring to Nirvâna,
Do passions pass away.

227. Old is this [adage], Atulo!
'Tis not as if to-day's:
The man who sitteth silently they blame,
They blame him speaking much;
They blame the man of measured words:
There's no one in the world unblamed.

228. There was not, won't be, is not now,
A mortal wholly blamed or wholly praised.

229. But one whom wise men,
     Knowing daily, praise,—
     Unblemished in behavior, clever,
     Steadfast in intellect and morals,—

230. Who dare blame him,
     Like unto finest gold?
     Him even angels praise;
     Yea, he is praised by the Most High.

231. Beware of bodily turbulence,
     In body be restrained;
     Renouncing ill conduct of body,
     Observe good bodily conduct.

232. Beware of turbulence of speech,
     And be in speech restrained;
     Renouncing ill conduct of speech,
     Observe good conduct therein.

233. Beware of mental turbulence,
     And be restrained in mind:
     Renouncing ill conduct of mind,
     Observe good mental conduct.

234. Restrained in body are the wise,
     Likewise in speech restrained;
     The wise are mentally restrained,
     Restrained all round are they.

XVIII. Banes

235. Now like unto a yellow leaf thou art,
    The messengers of Pluto wait on thee,
    Thou standest on the threshold of thine exit,
    And no provision for the journey hast.

236. Make for thyself an island,
    Work hard, be a scholar:
    With stains blown off, and free from guilt,
    The divine Aryan land thou shalt enter.

237. Thine age is consummated now,
    Departed art thou into Pluto's presence,
    Thou hast no halting-place upon the road,
    And no provision for the journey hast.

238. Make for thyself an island,
    Work hard, be a scholar:
    With stains blown off, and free from guilt,
    Never again into birth and old age thou shalt enter.

239. Gradually, little by little, moment by moment,
    Like a smith [with the dross] of silver,
    Let a wise man blow away the stains of self.

240. As the stain that hath its origin in iron
    Doth eat that only whence it had its rise,
    So the transgressor do his own deeds lead
    Unto the world of woe.

241. Omission is the bane of prayers:
    Of houses, laziness the bane;
    The bane of beauty, indolence;
    And carelessness the watchman's bane.

242. Ill conduct is a woman's bane,
    A giver's bane is avarice;
    A bane are all bad doctrines,
    In this world and the next.

243. Thence, more baneful than the rest,
    Is Ignorance, the bane supreme.
    This bane renouncing, baneless be, O monks!

244. Easy is life to live for a shameless man,
    Impudent as a crow, and backbiting,
    Aggressive, bold, depraved.

245. Hard is life for a modest man,
    Ever in quest of what is pure,
    Disinterested, retiring, clean-lived, clear-sighted.

246. He who destroyeth life and speaketh lies,
    Who taketh in the world what is not given,
    And goeth to another's wife;—

247. And the man who is addicted to strong drink,
    E'en in this world doth his own root dig up.

248. O mortal, know thou this:
    Evil is the state of the intemperate;
    Let not impiety and greed
    Reduce thee long to pain.

249. Folk give according to their faith,
    According to their fancy;
    Therefore whoe'er is sad at others' food and drink
    By day or night arriveth not at Trance.

250. But he with whom this [feeling] is cut off,
    Uprooted and removed,
    Surely by day or night
    Arrives at Trance.

251. There is no fire like passion,
    No monster like unto hate;
    There is no net like folly,
    No torrent like to Thirst.

252. Easy to see the fault of others,
    But hard one's own to see:
    His neighbor's faults as chaff one winnoweth,
    But hideth his own, as a cheating gambler his die.

253. In one who looketh for another's faults,
Conscious always of annoyance,
His passions grow:
From passional destruction he is far.

254. In air there is no path,
A philosopher is not external:
The crowd are quite contented with phenomena;
Beyond phenomena the Perfect Ones.

255. In air there is no path,
A philosopher is not external:
The constituents of existence are not eternal,
Immutable the Buddhas.

NOTES TO CHAPTER XVIII.

Chap. XVIII. "Banes" is a rendering of a word which also denotes dirt or stain.

235. "Pluto," *Yamo*, the president of departed spirits.

236. "Aryan," generally translated "Noble" or "Elect." It is a term of racial aristocracy, such as it has now become with us.

248. "Greed and impiety" is the order in the Pâli.

249, 250. It is verses like this, so evidently referring to the monastic life, that help us to interpret aright the allusions to the recitation of the sacred lore in such passages as Stanzas 259, 363.

254. "Perfect Ones," *Tathâgatâ*. This is a verse for the later Transcendentalists, who held that Buddha was beyond the world.

XIX. The Just

256. Because he carrieth the right by force,
    A man is not therefore just;
    But the scholar who can distinguish both right and
    wrong;—

257. Who leadeth others not by force,
    But by equal justice,
    Of justice guardian wise,
    He is called the just.

258. A man is not a scholar
    Because he speaketh much:
    He who is calm, unwrathful, fearless,
    He is called a scholar.

259. A man is not a reciter of the Doctrine
    Because he speaketh much:
    One who hath learnt but little,
    But seeth the Doctrine as a system,
    He is a reciter of the Doctrine,
    Who neglecteth it not.

260. A man is not an Elder
    Because his head is grey:
    Ripe though his age,
    He is called "Old in vain."

261. In whom there are truth and justice,
    Gentleness, temperance, control,
    The wise who is rid of stains,
    He is called an Elder.

262. Not by mere speech-making or fine complexion
    Is an envious, miserly, dishonest man handsome.

263. But he with whom this [evil] is cut off,
    Uprooted and removed,
    The wise man who is rid of hate,
    He is called handsome.

264. Not by shaving is an undisciplined,
    Mendacious man philosopher:
    Given up to desire and greed,
    Will he be a philosopher?

265. He who doth quiet evil things
    Of every kind, minute and big,
    By the quieting of evil things,
    He is called a philosopher.

266. A man is not a mendicant
    Because he lives by mendicancy:
    By taking into him the whole religion
    A man's a monk, not otherwise.

267. He who both merit and demerit
    In this world puts away,
    Living the life of religion,
    Who walketh in the world considerately,
    He is called a monk.

268. Not by silence is one a sage,
    Foolish and ignorant;
    But the scholar, holding the scales]
    And taking the best;—

269. Who shunneth evils, he is a sage,
    He is a sage thereby;
    Who weighs both worlds
    Is thereby called a sage.

270. A man is not an Aryan
    Because he hurteth living things:
    By hurting not all living things
    A man is called an Aryan.

271. Not by mere ritual,
    Nor again by many truths,
    Neither by gain of trance, nor lonely lodge,—

272. Reach I renunciation's bliss,
    The quest of the *élite*.
    O monk, be thou not confident
    While unattained is passional destruction.

NOTES TO CHAPTER XIX.

259. *Dhammadharo* is the regular word for a reciter of the Sûtras. "System" or "body." Such pregnant terms as this gave rise to fine-spun theories in later Buddhism.

260. "Elder," *Thero*, like the N. T. "presbyter."

265. To convey an idea of the punning etymology, which is so frequently found in ancient writings, one might translate thus:

> "He who saith *Fie!* to evil things,
> The *filer*-down of evil things,
> He is called a *phi*-losopher."

266. "Mendicant" and "monk" are two renderings of the same word *bhikkhu*, a religious beggar or friar.

XX. The Way

273. Of ways the best the Eightfold is;
Of truths, the stanzas four;
The best of doctrines is passionlessness;
The best of bipeds is the Seeing One.

274. This is the only Way;
No other is there for cleansing of insight:
Enter ye thereupon;
That [other] is the Tempter's blandishment.

275. Entered thereon, ye'll make an end of pain:
The Way was taught by me who knew
The remedy for thorns.

276. By you the effort must be made;
The Perfect Ones are teachers;
The thoughtful, entered on the path,
Will be delivered from the Tempter's bond.

277. Impermanent all compounds of existence!
When this one knows and sees,
Then he becomes averse to pain:
This is the way of purity.

278. Painful are all the compounds of existence!
When this one knows and sees,
Then he becomes averse to pain:
This is the way of purity.

279. Impersonal all mental states!
When this one knows and sees,
Then he becomes averse to pain:
This is the way of purity.

280. Whoever riseth not at rising time,
Young, strong, indulging sloth,
Weak in his mind's resolve, and indolent,
Pure Reason's way the slothful findeth not.

281. Watchful of speech and well restrained in mind,
     With body also let one do no wrong:
     Purify these three paths of act,
     Strive for the way made public by the Seer.

282. From zeal is wisdom born,
     By want of zeal 'tis lost:
     Knowing this twofold path of gain and loss,
     Let one conduct himself suchwise as wisdom groweth.

283. Cut down the forest, not a tree;
     Out of the forest fear is born:
     When felled are forest and desire,
     Then, monks! be fancy-free.

284. So long as desire is not cut off,
     Even the smallest, of a man for women,
     So long is such an one bound down in mind,
     Like the milch calf unto his dam.

285. Cut off self-love,
     E'en as an autumn lotus with the hand;
     Cherish the way of peace—
     Nirvâna, shown by the Auspicious One.

286. "Here will I live in the rains,
     There in the winter, [yonder] in the heats."
     So thinks the fool, awake not to his latter end.

287. A man solicitous for sons and cattle,
     With mind distraught,
     Doth Death bear off,
     As a flood the sleeping village.

288. Sons are no shelter,
     Nor are sires or kin:
     For him who is arrested by the Ender
     No shelter is there in his kinsfolk.

289. Knowing this reality,
     The scholar, restrained by ethics,
     Should quickly clear the way
     Which to Nirvâna goes.

NOTES TO CHAPTER XX.

273. The Noble Eightfold Way and the Four Noble Truths (or Axioms) are explained in Buddha's First Sermon. (S. B. E. Vol. XI., p. 137; XIII, p. 94)

281. *Isi* (Sanskrit *Rishi*) is a common name for a Buddhist, being transferred from the old Vedic seers. Samuel Beal regarded *Essene* as a Greek transliteration of it, on account of the singular coincidence of the double plurals in Pâli and Greek: *isayo, isino;Εσσαῖοι, Ἐσσῆνοι.*

283. "Forest" and "desire" are the same word. "Fancy-free" is literally "desireless," but according to some MSS. we read the word Nirvâna used adjectivally.

XXI. Miscellany

290. If by resigning some small happiness
     One see a larger one,
     Let a wise man resign the smaller one,
     Looking unto the larger happiness.

291. He who his own happiness wisheth
     By imposing pain on others,
     Entangled in entanglements of wrath,
     From wrath is not released.

292. What ought to be done is left undone,
     But what ought not to be done is done:
     The Depravities of the insolent and careless grow.

293. But those who ever strive to cultivate
     A mindfulness intent upon the body,
     What ought not to be done they follow not—
     The constant doers of what things should be done:
     Of those mindful and conscious ones
     The Depravities pass away.

294. Mother and father having slain,
     And two kings of the Warrior caste;
     A kingdom and its people having slain,
     A Brahmin scatheless goes.[17]

295. Mother and father having slain,
     And two kings of the Brahmin caste,
     Yea, and an eminent man besides,
     A Brahmin scatheless goes.

---

[17] This verse seems inexplicable. There was a law in ancient India forbidding a Brahmin to be executed even though he had committed the worst crimes. (Cf. S. B. E., Vol. II, p. 242; XIV, pp. 201, 233.) In alluding to this fact, the Buddhists attached a mystical meaning to it, saying that a monk has slain thirst (*tanhâ*) which is the mother and ignorance (*avijjâ*), which is the father of our bodily existence. The explanation of the two kings and one eminent man must be sought in a play on thoughts of the same kind.

For further details see Beal's *Translation 0/ the Chinese Dhammapada*, quoted in Carus's *Buddhism and its Christian Critics*, p. 190–191. The latter calls attention to the parallelism of this verse to Matth. X, 21. Luke's version is still more striking (Luke XII. 51–53).

296. Those disciples of Gotamo
    Waken with true awakening
    Whose mindfulness by day and night
    Is ever intent on Buddha.

297. Those disciples of Gotamo
    Waken with true awakening,
    Whose mindfulness by day and night
    Is ever intent upon the Doctrine.

298. Those disciples of Gotamo
    Waken with true awakening,
    Whose mindfulness by day and night
    Is ever intent upon the Order.

299. Those disciples of Gotamo
    Waken with true awakening,
    Whose mindfulness by day and night
    Is ever intent upon the body.

300. Those disciples of Gotamo
    Waken with true awakening,
    Whose mind by day and night
    Is delighted with gentleness.

301. Those disciples of Gotamo
    Waken with true awakening,
    Whose mind by day and night
    Is delighted with meditation.

302. Hard is the hermit life, hard to enjoy;
    Hard are the monasteries, painful are the houses;
    Painful is living together with unequals,
    And pain befalls the wayfarer:
    Therefore be not a wayfarer,
    Be not beset with pain.

303. The believer, graced with virtue,
    With glory and wealth his portion,
    Chooseth what place soe'er he may,
    And in that same place is worshipped.

304. The genuine shine afar,
    Like the Himâlaya mount:
    The false are not seen here,
    Like arrows shot by night.

305. Lone-sitting and lone-lying,
    Walking alone unwearied,
    Subduing self alone,
    Let one be gladsome in the forest glade.

NOTES TO CHAPTER XXI.

296-301. These stanzas all occur in the Prâkrit birch-bark fragments from Chinese Turkestan. The use of the family name Gotamo instead of the Master's religious titles is a mark of antiquity, just as "Jesus" in the Gospels indicates an older usage than the "Lord" of later times. In the Prâkrit text the word "always," which is found in the Pâli, is replaced by "these"—a reading preferred by Senart and adopted here.

302. The exigencies of the metre make it hard to decide whether "unequals" or "equals" be meant.

305. Literally "forest-end," a pun on "desire-end."

XXII. Hell

306. The sayer of what is not goes to hell,
And also he who doeth and saith "I did not";
Both when departed equal are:
In the next world they are men of abandoned deeds.

307. Many who wear the yellow robe
Are ill-natured and intemperate:
Evil by evil deeds, they are born in hell.

308. Better to eat the red-hot iron ball,
Like flame of fire,
Than for a man immoral and intemperate
To eat the kingdom's alms.

309. Four conditions do a reckless man,
Familiar with another's wife, befall:
Demerit's gain, uncomfortable bed;
Thirdly censure, and fourthly hell.

310. Demerit's gain and evil future state,
Brief rapture of the frightened man and woman;
The king imposeth heavy punishment:
Therefore let none frequent another's wife.

311. E'en as a grass-blade wrongly grasped
Doth cut the hand,
So doth the philosophic life, when wrongly taken up,
Drag down to hell.

312. Every perfunctory deed and vow corrupt
And faltering chastity, is no great fruit.

313. If aught is to be done, do that,
And do it with thy might:
A perfunctory hermit scatters dust the more.

314. Better undone a misdemeanor:
A misdemeanor afterwards torments;
Better done a good deed is,
Which done tormenteth not.

315. E'en as a frontier fort,
     Guarded within, without,
     So guard thyself; let not a moment pass:
     Lost moments mourn in hell, [whereto] consigned.

316. Beings who are ashamed of what is not shameful,
     But of the shameful thing are not ashamed,
     Embracing false belief, go to the world of woe.

317. Beings who fear when there is naught to fear,
     And when there is aught fear not,
     Embracing false belief, go to the world of woe.

318. Beings who shun what is not to be shunned,
     And shun not what they should,
     Embracing false belief, go to the world of woe.

319. Beings who know what should be shunned as such,
     And what need not be shunned as not to be,
     Embracing Right Belief, go to the world of bliss.

NOTE TO CHAPTER XXII.

315. Owing to the ambiguity arising from the fact that Pâli nouns and adjectives are interchangeable, this may mean that the losers of the moments mourn; but the compound word *khanâtîtâ* can hardly mean aught else than lost moments.

XXIII. The Elephant

320. Hard words I'll bear as bears the elephant
The arrow shot in battle from the bow,
For immoral are the vulgar.

321. They lead to conflict the tamed [elephant],
And the tamed the king doth mount:
Best among men the tamed,
Who hard words beareth.

322. Good are tamed mules and noble Indus horses,
And great-tusked elephants;
But better still a self-tamed man.

323. Not by such bearers may one go
To the untrodden bourn:
The tamed one goeth on the tamed,
To wit, upon a well-tamed self.

324. "Wealth-keeper" the elephant,
Savage, with temples running, hard to hold,
When bound no morsel eateth.
The elephant remembereth the elephant forest.

325. When one is torpid and gluttonous,
Sleepy, rolling about as he lieth,
Like a great corn-fed hog,
Unto a womb that stupid one
Is born again and again.

326. Once did this heart wander and roam
As it listed, where it liked, just as it pleased:
To-day completely shall I hold it in,
As a mahout the furious elephant.

327. In earnestness be joyful, guard the heart;
From the hard road extricate thyself,
As an elephant sunk in the mire.

328. If a prudent companion a man can get,
Who walketh with him, sober-living, wise,
With such let him walk, rejoicing and reflecting,
All dangers vanquishing.

329. If a prudent companion a man cannot get
     Who walketh with him sober-living, wise,
     Then, like a king who leaves his conquered kingdom,
     Must the outcast walk alone,
     As an elephant in the forest.

330. 'Tis better alone to walk:
     With a fool there is no fellowship;
     Walk alone and do no evils—
     An outcast, wanting little,
     Like an elephant in the forest.

331 When need ariseth, sweet is fellowship;
    Sweet is enjoyment when 'tis mutual;
    Sweet is a good life in the hour of death;
    Sweet the abandonment of every pain.

332. Sweet in the world is motherhood,
     And fatherhood is sweet;
     Sweet in the world the philosophic life,
     And sweet the Brahmin life.

333. Sweet is a moral life down to old age;
     Sweet is a settled faith;
     Sweet the attainment of intelligence;
     Not doing evil things is sweet.

NOTE TO CHAPTER XXIII.

324. Wealth-keeper," one of the names of an elephant that was set
to attack Buddha.

XXIV. Thirst

334. In a careless-living man
Thirst like a creeper groweth;
He runneth from life to life,
As a monkey in the woods in quest of fruit.

335. Whomever this vile world-wide Thirst o'ercomes,
His sorrows grow, like the o'ergrown kuss-kuss grass.

336. When one o'ercometh this vile Thirst,
So hard to conquer in the world,
Sorrows from him fall off,
As a water-drop from a lotus.

337. Well therefore say I unto you,
You who are gathered here,
Dig up the root of Thirst,
As he who wants the scented root
Digs up the kuss-kuss grass,
Lest the Tempter crush you again and again,
As the river the reed.

338. Even as while the root is safe and strong,
The tree cut down groweth up once again,
So while Thirst's inclination is not killed,
This pain returns repeatedly.

339. For whom strong waves, in six-and-thirty streams,
Are streaming unto pleasure,
That misbeliever do his purposes,
On passion set, bear on.

340. The streams flow everywhither,
The creeper sprouting standeth:
When ye have seen that creeper springing up,
Then cut the root by intellect.

341. Rushing and unctuous are a creature's joys;
In pleasure resting, seeking happiness,
Birth and old age men undergo.

342. Mortals who make Thirst their leader,
     Like hunted hare run to and fro;
     Bound in Fetters and bonds,
     Pain do they undergo long and repeatedly.

343. Mortals who make Thirst their leader,
     Like hunted hare run to and fro;
     Thirst therefore a monk should put away,
     Longing for his own passionlessness.

344. He who, free from desire, is inclined thereto,—
     Who, from desire delivered, runs to that very same,—
     Only behold that individual:
     He runneth into bondage when delivered.

345. The wise say not that bond is strong
     Which iron, wooden, hempen is:
     Far firmer is regard for gems,
     For ornaments, for sons and wives.

346. That bond the wise call strong
     Which, dragging loose, is hard to untie:
     When men have cut this too, they leave the world,
     Without cares, renouncing lust and ease.

347. Those who are dyed with passion follow
     The self-made stream, as a spider his web:
     When they have cut this too, wise men walk on
     Without cares, all pain renounced.

348. If thou wouldst cross to yonder shore,
     Give up the former and the latter things,
     And what is midmost:
     With mind on every side emancipated,
     Thou shalt not enter birth and old age again.

349. For a man distressed by conjectures,
     With passions vehement, observing what is fair,
     Thirst groweth more;
     He maketh bondage strong.

350. But he whose joy is quieting conjectures,
    Who, mindful always, contemplateth foulness,
    He will abolish, he will cut the Tempter's bond.

351. He who hath reached the consummation, undismayed,
    Devoid of Thirst and guiltless,
    The thorns of being he hath cut away:
    This complex form his last [will be].

352. Devoid of Thirst, without attachment,
    In etymology and metre skilled,
    Knowing the letters' order, first and last,
    He indeed doth his last body bear,
    He is called the Great of Intellect.

353. O'ercoming all and knowing all am I;
    By all conditions undefiled,
    Renouncing all, by Thirst's destruction freed,
    Having myself supremely understood,
    Whom may I teach?

354. The gift of truth o'ercometh every gift,
    The taste of truth o'ercometh every taste,
    Delight in truth o'ercometh all delight,
    And Thirst destroyed o'ercometh every pain.

355. Possessions kill the fool;
    But never those who seek the farther shore;
    The fool, by thirst of possession, killeth himself as others.

356. Weeds are the plague of fields:
    This race is passion-plagued.
    Therefore to give unto the passionless
    Hath great reward.

357. Weeds are the plague of fields:
    This race is plagued by hate.
    Therefore to give to those of hatred void
    Hath great reward.

358. Weeds are the plague of fields:
    This race is plagued by folly.
    Therefore to give to those devoid of folly
    Hath great reward.

359. Weeds are the plague of fields:
This race is plagued by wishes.
Therefore to give to those exempt from wishes
Hath great reward.

NOTES TO CHAPTER XXXIV.

353. This stanza was uttered by Buddha soon after his Enlightenment. (Sacred Books of the East, Vol. XIII, p. 91.)

354. "Truth," *dhammo.* Cf. Psalm cxix. 103.

355. The last line is literally rendered. It may mean either, "as well as others" (Fausböll); or, "as if others," i. e. "as if aliens" = "as if his own enemy" (Max Müller and Hû).

356. Cf. Mark ix. 41.

XXV. The Monk

360. Good is a continence of eye,
     A continence of ear is good;
     Good is a continence of nose,
     A continence of tongue is good.

361. Good is a continence of body,
     And good a continence of speech;
     A continence of mind is good,
     And good is continence every way:
     The monk in every way contained,
     From all pain is delivered.

362. Restrained in hand, in foot restrained,
     In speech restrained, restrained to the uttermost
     Delighting inwardly, composed,
     Alone, contented, him they call a monk.

363. The monk of mouth restrained,
     Reciting texts without conceit,
     Illuminates the meaning and the Doctrine:
     Sweet is the speech of such.

364. The Doctrine is his garden, his delight;
     On Doctrine thinking oft,
     The monk remembereth the Doctrine,
     And from the Gospel falleth not away.

365. His own share let him not despise,
     Nor walk in envy of others:
     The monk who others envieth
     Attaineth not to Trance.

366. If a monk should receive but little,
     His own share let him not despise:
     Him do the angels praise,
     When pure-lived, unremitting.

367. He who in no wise maketh Name and Form his own,
     Who mourneth not for that which is no more,
     He indeed is called a monk.

368. The monk who liveth in love,
    Convinced of the Buddha's religion,
    The happy place of peace may reach,
    Where stilled are life's constituents.

369. Empty, O monk, this boat:
    Emptied by thee, 'twill lightly go;
    When passion and hatred are cut away,
    Into Nirvâna thou shalt enter then.

370. Cut off the Five, renounce the Five,
    And practice Five besides:
    The monk escaping from attachments five
    Is called a flood-crossed one.

371. Be rapt, O monk, and be not careless,
    Let not thine heart in the sense-pleasures whirl,
    Lest, careless, thou the iron ball shouldst gorge,
    And burning cry: "'Tis pain!"

372. Unto the unintelligent no trance,
    Unto the unintranced no intellect:
    With whom there is both trance and intellect
    Truly is he unto Nirvâna nigh.

373. Unto the monk entering his empty house
    With heart at peace
    Delight unearthly is,
    To him who clearly seeth Doctrine true.

374. When one hath grasped
    Of Elements the origin and lapse
    He gains the immortal joy and ecstasy
    Of those who understand.

375. Now this is the beginning here below
    Unto a monk intelligent:
    Guarded faculties, contentment,
    And restraint under the Confessional;
    Cultivate lovely friends,
    Pure-lived and unremitting.

376. Let him be neighborly and well-mannered;
Then, in the fullness of ecstasy,
Will he make an end of pain.

377. E'en as the aloes sheds its withered flowers,
So, monks, both passion and hate shed ye.

378. Quiet in body and of quiet speech,
Mentally quiet and well composed,
The monk who this world's baits hath voided
Is called a Quietist.

379. By self exhort thyself,
Examine self by self:
Self-guarded and collected,
Thou shalt, O monk, live happily.

380. For self is lord of self,
Oneself is his own destiny:
Curb thyself therefore,
As a merchant a goodly steed.

381. A monk is full of ecstasy
When of Buddha's religion convinced;
The happy place of peace he may attain,
Where stilled are life's constituents.

382. The monk yet young
Who unto Buddha's religion devoteth himself,
Brighteneth this world,
As the moon from cloud set free.

NOTES TO CHAPTER XXV.

This chapter on the Monk necessarily relates to him technically, and one of his chief duties was to recite the Canon. See Stanzas 19 and 20, 259, and note to 249. The Prâkrit text, however, in Stanza 363, betrays a various reading: "speaking little" instead of "reciting Mantras."

363. *Mantabhânt*, "reciting Mantras," is rendered "speaking wisely," by Max Müller, Childers, Hû, and Fausböll. But this whole passage evidently relates to the recitation of the Dhammo.

365, 366. "His own share" refers to the portion for recitation. Monks were jealous about this. See Max Müller's note to Stanza 19.

370. The commentary, quoted by Fausböll, indicates that the last five mean the five moral faculties.

XXVI. The Brahmin

383. Cut off the stream by striving;
Drive out, O Brahmin, lusts:
When thou hast known, O Brahmin, the Constituents'
destruction,
Then art thou wise in what is increate.

384. When in two things (*dhammâ*)
The Brahmin to the farther shore hath gone,
All Fetters fall away from him who knows.

385. For whom the farther shore, the hither,
Or neither is not known,
Painless and fetterless,
Him do I call a Brahmin.

386. Rapt, blameless, settled, with his duties done,
Without Depravities, the highest goal attained,
Him do I call a Brahmin.

387. By day shineth the sun,
And night the moon illumes;
In armor full the warrior shines;
And rapt the Brahmin shineth;
But all the day and night
In splendor shines the Buddha.

388. When rid of evil one is called a Brahmin,
And by an even life philosopher;
Making the stain of self renounce the world,
Thereby. an hermit one is called.

389. No man a Brahmin should attack,
Nor should a Brahmin him revile:
Woe to the striker of a Brahmin,
More woe if this one him revile.

390. Unto a Brahmin better 'tis by far
When from things dear the mind is weaned;
Whene'er the mind turns back from injuring,
Then, then for certain pain is calmed.

391. For whom by body, speech and mind
     No misdemeanor is,
     In these three points restrained,
     Him do I call a Brahmin.

392. So soon as one the Doctrine understandeth,
     Taught by the thoroughly Enlightened One,
     Zealously let him worship it,
     As a Brahmin the fire of sacrifice.

393. Neither by braided locks, nor yet by clan,
     Nor birth, a Brahmin is;
     In whom both truth and Doctrine are,
     He is the blest, the Brahmin he.

394. Fool! Of what use to thee are braided locks?
     What use the goat-skin garb?
     Within thee there is ravening:
     The outside thou makest clean.

395. The man who weareth dusty rags,
     Emaciate, seamed with veins,
     Lone in the forest rapt,
     Him do I call a Brahmin.

396. A Brahmin no one do I call
     Womb-born, from [Brahmin] mother sprung;
     He may to men say, "Sirrah!"
     Wealthy indeed is he:
     The poor who is not grasping
     Him do I call a Brahmin.

397. Whoso, when every fetter is cut off,
     Doth tremble not,
     From ties escaped, unfettered,
     Him do I call a Brahmin.

398. Whoso hath cut the latchet and the strap,
     The rope and all concomitants,
     Hath thrown the cross-bar up, and is *awake* (*Buddha*),
     Him do I call a Brahmin.

399. Whoso, though innocent, endures abuse,
Yea, stripes and bonds,—
Patience his power, and power his army,—
Him I call a Brahmin.

400. Unwrathful and devout,
Virtuous, free from appetite,
Tamed, and indued with his last body,
Him I call a Brahmin.

401. He who, like water on a lotus-leaf,
Like mustard-seed upon an arrow-point,
Sticks not in lusts,
Him do I call a Brahmin.

402. Whoso e'en here doth know
Destruction of the pain of self,—
His burden fallen, the unfettered one,—
Him I call a Brahmin.

403. Profound in intellect and wise,
Skilled in what is and what is not the way,
The highest goal attained,
Him do I call a Brahmin.

404. Aloof alike from houscholders and homeless,
No house frequenting, frugal in his wishes,
Him do I call a Brahmin.

405. Putting away violence 'mid beings weak or strong,
Who slayeth not, nor slaughter causeth,
Him I call a Brahmin.

406. Among the intolerant tolerant,
Among the violent extinct,
Ungrasping among those who grasp,
Him do I call a Brahmin.

407. From whom both passion, hatred, pride,
Yea, and hypocrisy,
As mustard-seed from arrow-point are fallen,
Him do I call a Brahmin.

408. Kind and instructive speech he speaketh true,
    Whereby no one he may offend:
    Him do I Brahmin call.

409. Whoso in this world naught ungiven takes,—
    Whether 'tis long or short,
    Small, large, or good or bad,—
    Him do I Brahmin call.

410. For whom desires are known not
    In this world or the next,
    Desireless, fetterless,—
    Him do I Brahmin call.

411. For whom abodes are known not,
    By knowledge free from asking, How?
    Who hath fast hold of the Immortal,
    Him do I Brahmin call.

412. Whoso in this world merit, demerit both
    Transcends the bondage of,—
    Sorrowless, stainless, pure —
    Him do I Brahmin call.

413. Spotless as the moon, and pure,
    Serene and unperturbed,
    With pleasure's fount destroyed,
    Him do I call a Brahmin.

414. Whoso this quagmire, hard to pass, hath passed—
    Transmigration and folly—
    Crossed to the farther shore,
    Enrapt and guileless, free from asking, How?
    Clinging to naught—extinct—
    Him do I call a Brahmin.

415. Whoso in this world hath forsaken lusts,
    And homeless goeth forth,—
    The fount of lust destroyed,—
    Him do I Brahmin call.

416. Whoso in this world hath forsaken Thirst,
    And homeless goeth forth,—
    The fount of Thirst destroyed,—
    Him do I Brahmin call.

417. The human yoke renounced,
    The yoke divine transcended is,
    Yokeless of every yoke:
    Him do I call a Brahmin.

418. Delight renounced, and undelight,
    Cold, with substrata gone,
    The Hero, who hath mastered every world:
    Him do I call a Brahmin.

419. Who knoweth everywhere the vanishing
    Of beings, and their resurrection eke,
    He who hath no attachment,
    Auspicious One and Buddha:
    Him do I call a Brahmin.

420. Whose destiny the angels do not know,
    Nor genii nor men—
    Depravities destroyed—the Arahat:
    Him do I Brahmin call.

421. Whoso before, behind, and in the midst,
    Hath naught his own,
    Possessing nothing, clinging unto naught:
    Him do I call a Brahmin.

422. The taurine noble Hero,
    Victorious mighty Seer,
    Guileless, a graduate, yea, a Buddha:
    Him do I Brahmin call.

423. Who knoweth his anterior abodes,
    Who seeth heaven and hell,
    Who birth-destruction hath attained,
    The Sage, accomplished in supernal ken,
    With all accomplishments accomplished:
    Him do I call a Brahmin.

NOTES TO CHAPTER XXVI.

388. Punning etymologies again.

394. Cf. Zech. XIII. 4; Luke XI. 39.

395. The second line occurs in the Great Epic. (Max M.)

396. From here to the end we have a triple transmission of the text: viz., in the present book, in the Sutta Nipâto, and the Middling Collection. Line 3 is literally: "He is termed a Bho-caller," i. e., one who says *Bho* ("Sirrah") to every one, including Buddhas and kings, to show his social supremacy.

402. *Ohitabhâro*, with burden laid down (Itivuttaka 44). It is a favorite phrase, and recalls Christian's burden in Bunyan.

405, line 1. Literally, "laying aside the rod." Cf. Middling Collection, Dialogue 86, translated in *The Open Court*, 1900.

406, line 2. Literally, "extinct among rod-graspers." "Extinct" is perhaps too literal, but "mild" would spoil the force and the association with Nirvâna.

412. The Prâkrit fragment reads "Buddha" instead of "pure," which in Pâli or Prâkrit requires only the change of a single letter.

417. "Yokeless," i.e. fetterless or without attachment (*yogo*).

423. "Heaven and hell," or paradise and purgatory. Some scholars object to the terms heaven and hell in Buddhist eschatology, because of their Christian association with eternity. But now that Talmudic research and New Testament criticism have shown that the everlastingness, at least of hell, was by no means universally admitted among the founders of the Christian faith, any such objection is in part removed. It still holds good, however, with regard to heaven; for did not Gotamo interview the archangel Bakko, and inform him that his aeons of bliss would expire? Accordingly, I have generally rendered *Saggo* by "Paradise," but in this final flourish of rhetoric, "heaven" is pardonable.

Glossary of Pâli Buddhist Terms

The Arabic (originally Hindû) numbers refer to the stanzas; the Roman to the chapters. The references are exhaustive in the most important cases, but *passim* and *etc.* are also used to denote frequent or repeated use. In Pâli every noun can have an adjectival sense, so that it is difficult always to distinguish between *dukkho, pâpo,* the adjectives, and *dukkham, pâpam,* the nouns. In these two cases, however, the nouns, as often occurs, are simply the adjectives in the neuter gender.

In the notes I have given the abbreviated form of neuter words: e.g., *citta, pada,* for *cittam, padam.* The m here is only a true m when followed by a vowel or by p, b or m. Generally it is merely a light nasal. But in the case of masculine nouns I always give the full nominative form: e.g., *dhammo,* instead of the stem-form, *dhamma. Buddha,* however, is given for *Buddho,* because it is now an English word.

Âbhassaro, 200, angel of splendor.
abhiññâ, 423, supernal ken.
adhammo, 84, injustice.
akkharo, 352, letter (of the alphabet).
akusalam, 281, wrong.
anâsavo, 126, sinless. *See* âsava.
anatto, 279, impersonal. *See* attâ.
aññâ, 57, 96, knowledge.
anupâdâya, 89, when fancy-free (literally, not clinging).
apâyo, 423, hell (literally, departure).
apuññam, 309, 310, demerit. *See* puññam.
arahâ, VII, 164, 420 etc., Arahat (literally, worthy). It is the equivalent of the Christian word "Saint."
ârâmo, 188, temple garden; 364, garden. (Its primitive meaning of garden or park became changed into that of Buddhist monastery, because rich men endowed the Order with parks for residence).
ariyo, 22, 79, 164, 206, 208, elect; 190, noble; 236, 270, Aryan.
asabbho, 77, wrong.[18]
âsavâ, 9, 10, 89, 93, 94, 292, 293, 386, 420, depravities; 226, 253, passions; 253, 272, passional (in composition). Rhys Davids renders this by "Intoxicants."
âso, 97, desire.

---

[18] We have not pretended to give all the ethical synonyms for goodness, wickedness, desire, etc., or we could hardly stop short of a concordance.

attâ, 88, 157-159, 282, 355, himself; XII, 159, 163, 380, oneself; 15, 16, 84, 217, 291, own; 106, 107, 160, 161, 164, 165, 209, 239, 285, 305, 322, 323, 379, 380, 388, 402, self; 315, 327, 379, 380, thyself.

aṭṭhangiko maggo, 273, eightfold way (of Buddhist ethics).

âvâso, 73, 302, monastery.

avijjâ, 243, ignorance (the tenth and last of the Fetters that bind man to personal existence).

bhâṇavâram, 196, lection, recital.

bhâvanâ, 301, meditation.

bhikkhu, XXV and passim, monk; 266, mendicant, monk (*bis*).

bho, 396, Sirrah!

Brahmâ, 105, God; 230, Most High. (See my note on this name in *The Open Court* for April, 1900.)

Brahmaṇo, XXVI, etc., brahmin.

Buddho, XIV, 75, 255, 296, 368, 381, 382, 387, 419, 422, Buddha; 398, awake (its real meaning).

cetiyam, 188, memorial. (It afterwards came to mean a memorial tree.)

ceto, 39, thought; 79, heart.

cittam, III, 13, 14, 33, etc., 88, 89, 116, 154, 183, 326, 371, heart; 138, mind. (Rhys Davids says it means the emotional mind.)

cuti, 419, vanishing (i. e. passing from one existence to another).

devaloko, 44, 45, 177, angel-world.

devo, 30, 56, 94, 181, 224, god; 105, 230, 366, 420, angel. (The latter is a better translation than "god" in a Buddhist book. But in such early texts as this, which contain some popular elements, the word has hardly lost its Brahmin associations. Moreover, the style is poetic, and "gods" is often more forcible and fitting.)

dhammadharo, 259, reciter of the Doctrine (the regular term for one who knew by heart the Sûtra portion of the Canon: *dharo* means carrying).

Dhammapadam, 44, 45, Dhammapada; 102, line of the Doctrine. (It was, I believe, Rhys Davids, in his *American Lectures* of 1895, who first pointed out that the Dhammapada was a Hymn-book.)

dhammiko, 84, just.

dhammo, 1, 2, creature; 20, 64, 65, 70, 79, 86, 87, 115, 144, 190, 205, 242, 259, 273, 297, 363, 364, 373, 392, 393, doctrine (generally meaning the Buddhist religion as a system, and specifically the Sûtra portion of the sacred Canon); 353, condition; 257, 261, justice; 82, 176, law; 279, mental state; 46 nature; 167-169, 266, religion; 164, right (adj.); 24, righteous; 354, truth.

diṭṭhi, 164, 167, speculation (literally, sight or view).

duggati, 17, perdition; 240, 316-318, world of woe. (It is literally bad going, i. e. misfortune.)

dukkatam, 314, 391, misdemeanor (a technical term in the monastic discipline).

dukkho, painful; dukkham, pain; 1, 69, 117, 144, 153, 189, 191, 192, 201, 202, 207, 221, 248, 275, 277-279, 291, 302, 331, 338, 342, 347, 354, 361, 371, 376, 390, 402. (The word means both physical and mental pain, and is the regular Buddhist term for the suffering of finite existence.)

gandhabbo (Sanskrit gandharvas), 105, 420, genius.

gâthâ, 101, 102, poem. (Gâthâ, poetry, was one of the ancient Nine Divisions of the sacred Canon.)

gati, 310, future state; 380, 420, destiny.

gato, 296-299, intent (literally, gone. It is important because entering into the composition of the Master's titles: Sugato and Tathâgato.)

Gotamo, 296-301 (Sanskrit Gautamas, contracted into the stem-form Gautama by European usage. It was the family name of Buddha, answering to our Shakespeare, etc.)

icchâ, 74, desire.

iddhi, 175, miracle. (A good enough translation in poetry. See my note on this word in *The Open Court* for June, 1900.)

indriyam, 7, 94, 375, faculty.

isi, 281, seer. *See also* mahesi.

issariyam, 73, lordship.

jano, 99, worldling; 217, common folk.

jhânam, 181, 372, trance.

jhâyam, 395, rapt.

jhâyî, 23, meditative; 110, 111, 414, enrapt; 276, thoughtful; 386, 387, rapt.

kalyânam, 116, goodness.

kâmaguno, 371, sense-pleasure.

kâmo, 48, 83, 88, 99, 186, 187, 346, 383, 401, 415, lust.

kammam, 15, 16, 66–68, 71, 96, 127, 136, 173, deed; 217, affairs; 281, act.

kâsâvam vattham, 9, yellow garb.

kâyo, 259, system (literally body).

khandho, 202, finite element; 374, element.

khattiyo, 294, warrior caste; 387, warrior

kusalam, 53, 183, goodness.

kusalo, 173, good.

lâbho, 75, gain; 365, share.

maggo, XX passim, way. See also aṭṭhangiko maggo.
mahesi (i. e. mahâ isi), 422, mighty seer.
manaso, 348, 390, mind. (In 348 it occurs in composition, where a becomes â.)
mano, 1, 2, 96, 116, 218, 233, 280, 281, 284, 301, 361, 390, 391, mind; 234, mentally (in the instrumental case, *manasâ*).
mâno, 74, 94, 150, 407, pride (one of the Ten Fetters).
manto (Sanskrit mantras), 241, prayer; 363, text. (In Sanskrit the term is applied to the Rig Veda.)
Mâro, 7, 8 (untranslated); 34, 37, 40, 46, 57, 105, 175, 274, 276, 337, 350, Tempter.
micchâdiṭṭhi, 316-318, false belief.
micchâsamkappo, n, false resolve.
moho, 251, 358, 414, folly.
muni, 49, 268, 269, 423, sage.

nâmarûpo, 221, 367, name and form.
nekkhammam, 181, 272, renunciation.
nibbânam, 23, 32, 75, 134, 184, 203, 204, 226, 285, 289, 369, 372, nirvâna (literally extinction, i. e. of the germs that lead to physical or even transcendental existences).
nibbuto, 406, 414, extinct; 196, in Nirvâna.
nirayo, XXII, passim, 126, 140, hell. (Like the hell of the Zoroastrians, of the Jews at the time of Christ, and of Christ himself, it is terminable. Cf. Matthew v. 26; Luke xii. 59; also verses 47, 48.)
nirûpadhi, 418, with substrata gone.
nirutti, 352, etymology (one of the sciences of the Brahmins. In Buddhism it came to mean exegesis and even language or dialect).

pabbajito, 74, 184, 388, hermit.
pabbâjayam, 388, making [to] renounce the world.
pabbajjam, 302, hermit-life.
padam, 100, sentence; 101, 102, line; 273, stanza; 352, metre; 381, place.
pamsukûlam, 395, dusty rags.
pandito, VI, passim, scholar, pandit.
paññâ, 28, 38, 40, 59, 152, 229, 340, 372, intellect; 333, intelligence; 280, Pure Reason. (Caroline Rhys Davids prefers "science" or "philosophy" rather than "intellect" or "reason," saying that it is doubtful whether the word means a function or an aggregate of functioning, or both. Stanza 152 evidently makes it mean a function. Rhys Davids says *paññâ* represents higher wisdom over against empirical opinion, *ditthi*.)

paññavâ, 84, intelligent.
pañño, 375, intelligent; 403, in intellect.
pâpadhammo, 307, ill-natured.
pâpako, 66, evil; 78, wicked.
pâpo, pâpam, IX, passim, evil, wrong; 15, 17, 69, 71, 161, 165, 173, 176, 269, 330, 333, 388, evil; 116, 117, 183, wrong; 39, 267, 412, demerit.
papañco, 195, 254, phenomenon.
pâram, 85, yonder shore.
paribbajati, 415, 416, to go forth.
paribbâjo, 313, hermit.
parihânam, 32, to be lost (lit. loss).
parinibbati, 126, to go to Nirvâna.
parinibbuto, 89, attained Nirvâna.
pasâdo, 249, faith. (In prose I should render it "conviction," to distinguish it from *saddhâ*.)
pasanno, 368, 381, convinced.
Pâtimokkham, 185, 375, Confessional.
poriso, 97, soul.
pubbenivâso, 423, anterior abode.
puñño, puññam, 39, 196, 267, 412, merit; 116, 118, right; 16, 18, 122, good, goodness.
pûjâ, 73, honors (the regular Hindû word for worship).
puriso, 54, soul; 78, 152, man.

râgo, 13, 14, 202, 251, 339, 347, 349, 356, 369, 377, 407, passion;

saddhâ, 8, 144, 333, faith.
saddhammo, 38, 60, 182, 194, 364, gospel (literally, good doctrine, good religion).
saddhâ, 303, believer.
saggo, 126, 174, 178, paradise; 423 heaven.
sahâyâ, 331, fellowship.
sahâyatâ, 61, fellowship.
sahâyitâ, 330, fellowship.
sahitam, 19, 20, portion (i. e. portion of Scripture allotted for recitation. Its Sanskrit form Samhitâ means a sacred text).
samâdhi, 144, 249, 250, 271, 365, trance.
sâmaññam, 19, 20, 311, philosophic life.
sâmaññatâ, 332, philosophic life.
samano, 142, 184, 254, 255, 264, 265, 388, philosopher. (See my note upon this word in *The Open Court* for April, 1900.)
sambodhi-angâni, 89, articles of full Enlightenment.
sambuddho, 181, real Buddha.

samgho, 190, 194, 298, Order (i.e. the Buddhist Church or Brotherhood).

samhito, 100, composed.

samkappo, 74, imagination; 147, 280, resolve; 339, purpose. (Right Resolve is the second step in the Noble Eightfold Way.)

samkhârâ, (plural), 203, existence; 255, constituents of existence; 277, 278, compounds of existence; 368, 381, life's constituents; 383, constituents.

sammâditthi, 319, right belief (the first step in the Noble Eightfold Path).

sammâsambuddho, 59, fully Enlightened One; 187, real Buddha; 392, thoroughly Enlightened One.

sammâsamkappo, 12, right resolve.

sampajo, 293, conscious.

samsâro, 60, 95, 414, transmigration; 153, to transmigrate.

samyogo, 384, fetter.

samyojanam, saññojanam, 221, 342, 397, fetter.

saññato, 104, restrained.

saññî, 253, conscious.

santavâ, 378, mentally quiet.

sappurisâ (plural), 83, the good.

sappuriso, 208, upright soul.

saranam, 188, 189, 190, 192, refuge.

sâsanam, 164, 183, 185, 368, 381, 382, religion.

sassato, 255, eternal.

sati, 293, 296-299, mindfulness (closely allied to conscience).

satîmâ, 91, thoughtful.

sato, 293, 350, mindful.

sâvako, 59, 75, 187, 195, 296–301, disciple.

sayam, 347, self.

sekho, 45, disciple (novice).

sîlabbatam, 271, ritual (the second of the Ten Fetters, including all kinds of external religiosity).

sîlam, 55, 57, 217, 303, virtue; 333, moral life; 144, 229, morals; 289, ethics.

sîlâni (plural of foregoing), 10, morals.

sîlavâ, 56, righteous; 84, moral; no, 400, virtuous.

sotâpatti, 178, entering the Path.

subho, 349, fair.

Sugato, 285, 419, Auspicious One (literally, well gone).

suggati, 18, bliss; 319, world of bliss.

tanhâ, XXIV, passim, 187, 251, 416, thirst; 180, desire.

Tathâgato, 254, 276, Perfect One. (This word is really untranslatable, and much has been written about it. *Gato*, "gone," is a word of

many associations, and among them is that of destiny. The Tathâgato is the Man of Destiny.)
thero, 260, 261, elder.

upapatti, 419, resurrection (i.e. re-birth, whether physical or transcendental).
upasampadâ, 183, initiation.
upasanto, 378, Quietist (literally, calmed).

viññânam, 41, consciousness. (It is here used as an adjective in the masculine, viññâno.)
viriyam, 7, 8, 112, will; 144, power of will.
visamkhâram, 154, eternity (literally, the non-composite).
vitakko, 349, 350, conjecture. (This is its Sanskrit meaning, but its general one in Pâli is conception or incipient mental activity.)
vîtarâgo, 99, passionlessness.
vivcko, 75, 87, seclusion.

Yamaloko, 44, 45, Hades.
Yamo, 235, 237, Pluto.
yogo, 23, yoga; 209, abstraction; 282, zeal; 417, yoke.

Postscript

Stanzas 3-6 are in the Middling Collection, Dialogue 128. which, though bearing the imprint of 1900, has only just been issued by the Pâli Text Society. The verses refer to the famous quarrel among the monks at Kosambi.

Stanzas 176 and 308 are found in the Chinese Middling Collection, Sûtra 14 (corresponding to No. 61 in the Pâli). The Chinese version was translated by Sylvain Lévi in 1896. That profound scholar points out that the title of this Sûtra among Asoko's Rock Edicts indicates a Prâkrit rather than a Pâli original. Moreover the Dhammapada stanzas, which must have been in the ancient original translated into Chinese in 397, are absent in the Pâli. But they probably were formerly therein, and were taken thence into our Hymns. The Chinese, however, agrees in the main with the Pâli, so that we are carried back at a single bound into the fourth century. The fortunes of the Canon before that period are still under debate, but there can be no doubt about the pre-Christian antiquity of the staple of it.

THE END

Made in the USA
Monee, IL
25 September 2022